5 WAYS FOR KIDS TO GROW

5 WAYS FOR KIDS TO GROW

By

Dashawn BillBill Johnson

© 2023 by D. Johnson

All rights reserved. This book or any portion

thereof may not be reproduced or used in any manner whatsoever without the express written permission of the publisher, except for the use of brief quotations in a book review.

ISBN: 978-1-7377923-4-5

About the Book

The child development approach is one that focuses on the social, emotional, mental, physical, and cognitive development of students. At the core of such an approach, the goal of education is to develop future citizens and lay the foundations for each child to realize their potential. "Five Ways for Kids to Grow" supports this approach and argues that every child in every school and community should be healthy, safe, engaged, supported, and challenged.

The steps outlined in this book can be used to develop school improvement processes that ensure the approach is integrated and systematized into schools and community processes and policies. These steps are not intended to be separate from academic development but rather to expand what academic development entails in this century and focus on all the attributes necessary for children's academic and social development and success.

TABLE OF CONTENTS

INTRODUCTION 7

CHAPTER 1 11

   Step One: Establish Your Growth 11

CHAPTER 2 24

   Step Two: Explore Careers You May be Interested In 24

CHAPTER 3 34

   Step Three: Networking 34

CHAPTER 4 52

   Step Four: Being Confident and Embracing Repetition 52

CHAPTER 5 63

   Step Five: Staying Active in Various Ways 63

Being active always 66

5 Ways for Kids to Grow / D. Johnson / 6

5 Principles to Succeed and Grow with 71

CONCLUSION..80

INTRODUCTION

Hello, young entrepreneurs, doctors, counselors, and good citizens. I know your future is bright, and you can't wait to live it up. Be all you can be, absolutely. On your path to success, I want to break down five simple steps that you will eventually have to take. These five ways will help you grow into the best person you can be. I followed these five steps and turned out quite alright.

The early years lay the foundation of a child's development. From junior high to high school, growth happens faster than at any later stage of life. During this time, the brain undergoes some of its most dramatic growth, and children gain the ability to enhance their thinking, speaking, learning, and reasoning skills. Early experiences can influence the physical architecture of the brain, shaping the neural connections in a child's developing brain.

Learning social and emotional skills will help you make friends and express your thoughts and feelings. As a kid, remaining calm, focused, and attentive will enable you to participate with others in activities that effectively promote verbal and non verbal skills.

In turn, learning from your mistakes by evaluating your reasoning and remembering the steps you took will strengthen your cognitive abilities. Ensuring that you come to school ready to learn has become a national priority. As a kid you have the opportunity to make a significant and lasting impact on your success and development by implementing what you learn to support the healthy social-emotional development of your wellbeing. This book explains what can happen when you come into contact with emotions and what actions can be taken to support your healthy social-emotional development.

5 Ways for Kids to Grow / D. Johnson / 10

CHAPTER 1

Step One: Establish Your Growth

Growing up is an exciting journey, full of new experiences and discoveries. As kids, you have incredible potential to grow in various aspects of your life. In this chapter, we will explore four important ways for kids to establish growth: physical, cognitive, social, and emotional development. Once you are able to identify your strengths and weaknesses in these four components, you will be able to develop new habits, determine ways to overcome your weaknesses, and witness the growth you have established. Let's dive in!

Physical Development

Physical development refers to the changes that occur in your body as you grow. It includes things like growing taller, gaining strength, and developing coordination. Here are some simple ways to promote physical growth:

Active Play: Engage in activities like running, exercising, and playing sports to strengthen your muscles, bones, and heart.

Healthy Habits: Eating foods with a good source of nutrients, getting enough sleep, and staying hydrated are also essential for your physical growth. Make sure to include fruits, vegetables, whole grains, and protein in your meals while limiting the intake of sugary snacks and drinks.

Action plan

- ✓ Make a list of the activities you can do to develop yourself physically.

- ✓ Engage in those activities, and if you need any help engaging in them, talk to friends, teachers, or family for help.

Reflective Question

- ➢ What are some activities that you have learned about?

➢ Where do you think you need to begin?

Cognitive Development

Cognitive development refers to the growth of your thinking and learning abilities. It involves developing skills such as problem-solving, memory, attention, and creativity. Here are some simple ways to enhance your cognitive growth:

Reading and Storytelling: Read books, listen to stories, and tell your own stories. This will help you improve your vocabulary, imagination, and understanding of the world around you. Visit your local library and choose books that interest you.

Puzzles and Games: Engage in puzzles, board games, and educational apps that challenge your mind. They will sharpen your problem-solving skills, critical thinking, and logical reasoning. Have fun while exercising your brain!

Curiosity and Exploration: Ask questions, observe things, and explore new ideas. Being curious about the world will expand your knowledge and encourage you to learn more. Visit museums, science centers, and zoos to satisfy your curiosity as well.

Action plan

- ✓ Ask your family or guidance counselor to get you some new books, puzzles, quizzes, and games that will help you develop your thinking ability.

- ✓ Learn how to play the games, practice, and master the games.

- ✓ Read the books; try to connect the books with your life in some type of way.

Reflective Question

➤ What are some things you want to learn about?

➤ What are some things you think you need to learn about to enhance your cognitive skills?

Social Development

Social development involves learning how to interact with others, cooperate, and make friends. Here are some simple ways to foster your social growth:

Communication Skills: Practice good communication skills by listening carefully and expressing yourself clearly. Use polite words, take turns in conversations, and show respect for others' opinions. Remember to use your words to resolve conflicts peacefully.

Teamwork and Collaboration: Engage in activities that require teamwork, such as group projects or team sports. Learning to work with and support your peers will help you develop valuable social skills and build strong relationships.

Volunteer and Help Others: Find opportunities to help others in your community. Volunteer at your school or church, participate in community service projects, and assist your family and friends when they need support. Being kind and helpful toward others teaches you empathy, compassion, and the importance of giving back.

Action plan

- ✓ Learn to listen carefully and don't give an immediate response to all inquiries.

- ✓ Collaborate with people to accomplish a task.

Reflective Questions

- ➢ How will you support others and help your community?

➢ What skills will you need to help others?

Emotional Development

Emotional development involves understanding and managing your feelings, as well as developing empathy toward others. Here are some simple ways to nurture your emotional growth:

Self-expression: Express your feelings through art, music, or writing in a journal. Drawing, painting, or playing an instrument can be great outlets for your emotions. Remember, it's okay to feel different emotions, like being eager, sad, angry, or happy. Expressing those emotions will help you understand yourself better.

Positive Relationships: Build healthy relationships with your family, friends, and teachers. Talk to them about your feelings, and listen to theirs. Being kind and understanding toward others helps you develop empathy and emotional intelligence.

Mindfulness and Relaxation: Take time to relax and practice mindfulness. Deep-breathing exercises, meditation, or yoga can help you calm your mind and manage stress.

Being aware of your emotions and taking care of your well-being is important.

Action plan

✓ Reflect back on the emotions you felt for the day.

✓ Take responsibility for your emotions and actions.

✓ Write about how you can manage those emotions.

Reflective Questions

➢ How do you view yourself in the future if you do/don't manage your emotions?

➤ What qualities do you look for in friends? Why is this important?

Develop your Expertise

This is a time when you should challenge yourself to strive for excellence in everything you do. Commit to working hard and achieving your goals. Once you begin to see progress, you will get a boost of confidence. Exploring your curiosity for things such as space travel, getting a pilot's license, building a hovercraft, creating a poetry book, or becoming a chess master could set you apart from others.

CHAPTER 2

Step Two: Explore Careers You May be Interested In

It's never too early to start thinking about your career. Take the time to explore different professions that pique your interest. You can conduct online research, read books, or engage in conversations with professionals in the fields that interest you. Finding out what you are passionate about early on will help you set goals and work toward achieving them. Learn about financial management, discuss various career paths with others, attend career fairs, and participate in job-shadowing opportunities. Remember, this is an exciting time to discover your interests and start building a foundation for your future.

Action Plan

- ✓ Make a list of careers that you are curious about or interested in.

- ✓ Research each career to learn more about what it involves and the skills required.

- ✓ Talk to family members, friends, or teachers who work in those fields and ask them questions.

- ✓ Attend career fairs or events in your community to gain hands-on experience and learn from professionals.

- ✓ Consider volunteering or interning in a field that interests you to gain practical knowledge.

Reflective Questions

- ➢ What are some careers that you have learned about and find exciting?

- ➢ Which skills do you think would be important in those careers?

➢ How can you gain more knowledge and experience in your chosen career path?

Engage and lead purposefully

You should go beyond the classroom to explore and develop your passions in academics, art, music, drama, social studies, athletics, and more. But does that mean you should join any extracurricular activity or club just because it looks good on your resume? Not at all. You must commit to the talents and interests that are important to you. For focused participation and leadership:

- Discover the many activities inside and outside your school. Your youth is an excellent time to try new and different experiences. Explore broader opportunities that align with your interests.

- Take steps to lead and contribute in a meaningful way. When you discover activities you enjoy, invest your time and energy in growing your skills in them. It's hard to master, but it's an important way to learn.

- Give back through service. Ask yourself: What do others need, and how can I help them?

Support makes it important to you

Try to understand different perspectives and step in when you see classmates being bullied or treated unfairly. Keep your promises. While this book encourages you to think big, it's important that you come up with a balanced plan that energizes you. Be careful not to overload. It is important to follow through on the tasks you chose to commit to. Each time, work on setting goals for academic and extracurricular activities and deciding which activities you can participate in.

Access your skills and abilities

Understand that you can help yourself determine what is the best fit for your career. Working and developing the skills you need to fit into a field that suits your strengths and choosing a career option that you can transition into naturally will increase your chances of success. Focus on a career that matches your current skills, as this will guide you in the areas you need to work on to be professionally ready.

Research your potential profession

When researching potential careers, it can be helpful to evaluate multiple careers at once so you can compare the career opportunities that are more suitable for you. By researching your areas of interest, you can also explore all the career paths you think are suitable and then decide which ones are best for you.

Determining the right profession

To determine if a skill is right for you, it's important to understand the expectations of those in the field. Researching the career requirements of the skill you're considering will help you better understand what you need to do to get into the field and what you need to do for success once you start your profession. Online research is a tool that allows you to learn more about what it takes to work in your chosen profession and grow.

Learn from existing professionals

An effective way to learn about your career is to talk to professionals who have already entered the field. If you know someone who works in the career you're considering or have contact information, asking them about their experiences can give you a first-hand idea of what it's like to work in that field.

Visit the workplace in person to learn

Visiting a workplace in person is a great way to learn more about working in a particular field. This could include finding a skill with little involvement in the field, such as an entry-level skill. You can also ask to shadow a professional in the field, follow them for a day or more, and see what their skills looks like on the path you envision.

CHAPTER 3

Step Three: Networking

Networking may sound like a big word, but it simply means building connections and relationships with people who can help you along your journey. These people could be teachers from your school, mentors, family, friends, or even professionals in your field of interest. Networking is important because it allows you to learn from others, gain valuable advice, and open doors to new opportunities. Attend community events, join clubs or organizations related to your interests, and be proactive in meeting new people. Always remember to be polite, show genuine interest in others, and be willing to help and support those around you. Networking is a lifelong skill that can greatly benefit you in both your personal and professional lives.

Action Plan

✓ Identify people in your community who can help you with your goals, such as teachers, mentors, family, or friends.

✓ Practice introducing yourself and engaging in conversation with new people.

- ✓ Attend community events, join clubs, or participate in extracurricular activities to meet new people.

- ✓ Seek advice and guidance from experienced people in fields that interest you.

- ✓ Be a supportive friend and offer help to others in your network.

Reflective Questions

- ➢ Who are some people in your community who can support you in achieving your goals?

- How can networking help you learn new things and open doors to opportunities?

- How can you contribute and be helpful to others in your network?

Connect with people

As a kid, you can learn a lot by reading books and conducting research, but often the real magic of what you learn comes from interacting with other people—asking questions, being curious, seeking understanding, and offering your help.

It is your responsibility to interact with people and stay in contact

Stay in close contact with people who work in the field you are interested in. Stand out, so other leaders will want to be around you. Watch educational videos on the different leadership styles if needed. Consistent communication will help you build stronger relationships with others, ultimately leading to a broader support system.

As you connect with other kids, you may get a chance to meet some of the professionals in their support system, which can increase your success and growth rate.

You can spend time learning with other kids. You should encourage yourself to keep in touch with other young scholars to offer and receive support as each of you gains new experiences and learns to reach your full potential. Try to bring your peers together by starting an educational club that you all can benefit from, such as learning about common talents, academics, and professional interests. Meet people who are different from you. In the coming years, you will undoubtedly meet classmates, teachers, program staff, and even young researchers who have different backgrounds or perspectives than you. Meeting people who are different than you is a great way to take advantage of opportunities to get out of your comfort zone and adapt to diversity.

Contribution to the world

You can contribute to the world through the important achievements and daily actions you are taking. You should try to discover the unique contributions—big ones—you can bring up to make the world a better place.

Ask yourself these questions:

- What do I want to achieve this year?

- How can I use my efforts and talents to benefit those I care about?

- What big idea can I work on?

- What problem can I solve, no matter how long it takes?

- What will be my legacy?

Your responsibility to contribute to the world is to:

Think big: Start today. Engage in purposeful exercises in your youth to define clear goals and specific steps you will follow to make progress.

This means that to be successful, you must do your best to learn and develop with every opportunity, skill, and more. Do things that allow you to be your best self so that you can contribute.

Identify the values, traits, and skills you can add to your footprint in the world. Discover your strengths and build on them. Identify your growth areas and make improvements. Let go of your lingering weaknesses, and accept that you are able and will take the steps to achieve your goals.

As a young star, you are given an extraordinary opportunity to help yourself now and in the future. You can contribute to the world in many different ways by reading and taking the right action.

- Use your skills to generate ideas, research, and make improvements to grow.

- Talk to the people you have included in your support system about your ideas and endeavors, and ask them for advice.

- Use your conversations with friends to expand and reflect on your plans.

- Get people excited to work with you to take the critical steps needed to achieve your Think Big goals.

Behavior and disciplinary policy

You are the leader of tomorrow. There will be many people observing your character to see how you handle situations, show concern for the communities, maintain a good disciplinary record, and work collaboratively with others.

Your education

You should know that being seen as smart is not as valuable as trying to learn and grow every day. The conscious pursuit of knowledge and skills is up to you.

What does this mean? Take control of your learning process. Figure out what works for you. Focus your energy on making the most of your educational opportunities.

Your learning responsibilities are as follows:

- Choose a skill or method that will allow you to grow and stretch. Use your resources to collaborate effectively. Talk to yourself about which factors are most important to your education.

- Make a plan that will prepare you. You must work on your plans to connect your goals and activities and enrich yourself with experiences that will help you coordinate your plans.

- Challenge yourself with the right rigorous objects and activities. Your plans should prepare you to be successful.

- Develop your research, writing, collaboration, and critical thinking skills. No matter what field or industry you want to work in, you need these skills to be an effective leader.

- Participate in contests, competitions, science fairs, mentorships, and other opportunities to gain "real world" experience and creative feedback outside of the classroom.

- Immerse yourself in a number of enriching learning experiences.

Habits and study tips for successful learning

As a kid, you have to work hard at your subject, and the commitment you put into it is all-important. You have to be willing to work to ensure that you become highly educated and proficient in your profession. Whatever challenges you face in the learning process and the difficulties you face in overcoming them will be worth it when you reach your goal and achieve what you want.

Therefore, you should acquire all the valuable habits and adequate study conditions that will help you study better and become the best student you can be.

As a kid, you may prefer to study with other students in a study group, while others may prefer to be free from distraction and study alone. Study groups are an excellent way to exchange ideas and learn more information. However, if your fellow students aren't as focused as you, studying alone can keep you from getting distracted.

You must find the best method for you because there will be a lot of things you will be required to know during the learning period. Don't be afraid to try new study methods to help you find what works best for you.

An essential part of learning is being organized, and making sure you manage your priorities and time is paramount. You'll need to learn how to stay organized and plan your priorities well. Every step you take must be put in order. Taking good steps now is an important habit to have as a successful, growing kid. Habits like giving yourself extra time to cover harder topics, sorting your study material, generally being punctual with timelines, and other life organization skills are important. All these areas will help you be well-prepared to become who you want to be.

Accepting help from mentors is another habit that students should acquire to develop their skills and become well-educated kids. There is real value in taking advantage of your education and career readiness. There is nothing wrong with asking your mentor for help so you can get another insight on what to work on. Study advisors, professors, and teaching assistants are the mentors you can turn to for guidance during your studies.

CHAPTER 4

Step Four: Being Confident and Embracing Repetition

Confidence is key to everything you do. Believe in yourself and your abilities, even when faced with challenges. Remember that it's okay to make mistakes and that falling short is an opportunity to learn and grow. Practice self-affirmations, surround yourself with positive influences, and celebrate your achievements, no matter how small. Another important aspect of growth is embracing repetition. Practice makes perfect, and by consistently working on your skills and goals, you will improve over time. Whether it's playing a musical instrument, studying for a test, or mastering a sport, dedicating time and effort to repetitive tasks will lead to great results. So keep practicing, stay determined, and never give up!

Action Plan

- ✓ Practice positive self-talk and affirmations to boost your confidence.

- ✓ Surround yourself with positive influences, such as friends who support and encourage you.

- ✓ Celebrate your achievements, no matter how small they may seem.

- ✓ Set goals for yourself and work on them consistently, even if it requires repetition.

- ✓ Embrace challenges as opportunities to learn and grow.

Reflective Questions

- ➢ What are some ways you can boost your confidence and believe in yourself?

➢ Who are the people in your life who encourage and support you?

➢ How can repetition and practice help you improve in different areas of your life?

Being consistent will increase your experience, skills, and confidence.

The repetition of reading a story over and over again or studying for futurology gives kids the practice they need to learn new skills. Repetition will help you increase speed, strengthen connections in the brain, and will help you learn. Confidence is the basis of all great successes.

Self-confidence is important in almost every aspect of our lives, but many people struggle to find it.

Ask yourself this:

- How can you be more confident?

- What is your life like now, and how different would it be if you increased your self-confidence?

The more confident individuals, managers, entrepreneurs, and businesses are, the more successful they are and the happier they are in their personal and professional lives. There is one thing you can do to have something in common with these individuals: Set small, achievable goals—this will help you move forward one step at a time.

You are capable of developing self-confidence. There is no one-size-fits-all approach to boosting self-confidence—your path to getting there will be as varied as you are. You must like challenges; for example, in a classroom, compete with other kids on who will become first at something, enjoy your work, and keep learning. You gain a life skill—the ability to build and restore your confidence.

Building confidence means trying something new without being afraid and knowing that you are succeeding at all times. As you learn, you grow, and your confidence increases.

So, try something new as an experience. When you play a game, double how much you practice, and don't forget to have fun with it! The main thing is to act! When you challenge yourself, something in your brain triggers, and your work becomes easier and more fun…and when you ask yourself, "What if?" Don't get caught up in that thought. Look for all the possibilities that could go wrong and work out ways to avoid them!

When you decide to do something and then actually set out to achieve it, you prove to your mind that you are capable and able, and it boosts your confidence! And the way to grasp this new skill and get it deep into your brain is to do it over and over again…repetition will help with mastery!

Practice, practice, practice makes perfect…

So now it's your turn…what do you choose? Decide how you want to challenge yourself with something new, and go for it! Sewing? Growing tomatoes? Cooking a good meal? Is it skydiving? Do you commit to daily meditation?

When you approach these types of life changes with a passionate attitude, you're less likely to stress or beat yourself up when things don't happen on time. You can approach taking on new challenges like a science experiment by setting a goal with plans on how to accomplish it in a timely manner. Spend time analyzing your progress and taking notes in a journal. Progress is approached with genuine curiosity about how things work. It automatically prompts you to ask yourself: What are you learning? What would you do differently next time? How do you approach it from a different perspective?

These are all good questions to ask yourself. And you don't have to go into much detail; you can take a few minutes each day to review where you are and where you want to be. Be patient with yourself as you train your brain for confidence! Be kind to yourself, think positively about your situations, and remember that it's all about the learning opportunities. No learning opportunity is ever wasted. Eventually, you will see your confidence grow, and you will soon discover the beautiful, powerful light within yourself.

CHAPTER 5

Step Five: Staying Active in Various Ways

Staying active doesn't just mean physical exercise, although that is important for your overall well-being. It also means staying engaged in activities that stimulate your mind and expand your horizons. Reading is a fantastic way to grow intellectually and develop a love for learning. Choose books that interest you, explore different genres, and visit your local library to discover new worlds through literature. Volunteering, keeping a social connection with your support system, and consistently eating mindfully are other ways you can stay active. Additionally, engaging in physical activities like working out, practicing yoga, or going for walks can help.

Action Plan

- ✓ Make a reading list and schedule regular reading time each day.

- ✓ Explore different genres of books and challenge yourself to try new ones.

- ✓ Engage in physical activities that you enjoy, such as playing sports, dancing, or riding a bike.

- ✓ Set aside time for quiet reflection or meditation to calm your mind and reduce stress.

- ✓ Get involved in your community by volunteering for local events, or joining clubs or organizations that align with your interests.

Reflective Questions

- ➢ What are some books or genres you want to explore?

- ➢ How does physical activity make you feel? What activities do you enjoy the most?

➢ How can quiet reflection or meditation help you in your daily life?

➢ In what ways can you contribute to your community through volunteering or joining clubs or organizations?

Being active always

There are many ways you can be active; it doesn't matter what you do or where you do it, as long as it's beneficial to you. The main thing is to have fun and enjoy it; it will be much easier to engage in. It's also good to break down your activities so you don't find yourself becoming overwhelmed. Every action you take matters!

Other ways to move are:

- To play sports

- Swimming

- Cycling

Try new activities and learn new skills, too, like:

- Create a sense of accomplishment.

- Increase your confidence to make more changes in your life.

If you want to learn fitness, try incorporating vigorous activities such as jogging, fast-paced sports, and strength training into your weekly routine; all these activities will make your body and brain active and make you ready during critical times.

Find activities you like:

Being more active can simply mean spending more time doing what you love, like gardening or visiting your local museum. Join a local sports, recreation, or fitness club; meet a friend for a walk or bike ride. Go talk to a friend for half an hour to learn some active ideas. Once you've found something you love, you're more likely to stick with it.

Be prepared to be active

It's important to be active and never too late to start, no matter what stage of life you're at—whether you're older, haven't been active for a while, or are just starting.

What success looks like

Success can be seen as personal fulfillment and happiness derived from pursuing one's passions and living a balanced life. It wears the cloak of self-belief, empowering individuals to push beyond their limits and reach new heights. It radiates confidence, standing tall amid challenges and setbacks. Success is a tapestry woven with personal growth, fulfillment, and a sense of purpose. It is not merely a destination but a lifelong journey encompassing various aspects of life, including professional achievements, personal relationships, and inner contentment.

Even when you struggle, the work you do benefits and touches people. You can always enjoy the effects of service by helping your peers, and there is clear evidence that supporting others can help ease negative emotions around you.

Ultimately, although success and happiness are linked. Pursuing success without also focusing on happiness and contentment may result in lives that are out of balance, with high levels of achievement but little in the way of personal fulfillment. But working on your happiness gives you the best chance of getting both.

5 Principles to Succeed and Grow with

1) **I can do anything:** Keep that mindset and continue to learn from your mistakes, and you will become the best version of yourself. If you don't give up, all your struggles in business, career, and health will eventually lead to success and happiness.

2) High motivation: No one can stop me: You strive to move forward and achieve your goals, and yet there seems to be no end to the obstacles and roadblocks in your path, so it is good if you feel there are none. You can stop to rest or regroup, but don't give up. When your motivation starts to falter, stop and think about the dream lifestyle you're fighting for and why it's so important to you. You see, it's that dream—your dream—

that fuels your motivation and gives you the strength to carry on, no matter what life throws at you. There are things you want and things you don't need to create the lifestyle you want, and they're all out of reach right now. But that doesn't mean you can't have them live the lifestyle of your dreams. You just haven't gotten there yet.

You won't get there without a firm commitment to achieving your goals. From where you are today to where you want to be in the future, you need a specific step-by-step plan, or you won't get there. You won't get there without taking steps toward your plan. And you can't do it without the drive and perseverance to fight adversity.

3) I can see the big problem inside the little figure: Everyone has problems, but how do you deal with them? I think it's a good concept. It takes a strong person to be bigger than your problems. Every problem is as big or small as you make it. Some people have nothing and yet are happy, and some people who have everything are unhappy.

With every problem that arises, there are only three things you can do:

1. Complain and do nothing.

2. Accept it and move on.

3. Accept it and do something to change it.

While you are learning, ask yourself what you can do to become bigger than your current state. Meet people who have a positive outlook, believe in overcoming obstacles, and challenge themselves to do better. Your mindset creates your reality. With a positive mindset, everything will always go well, and you will always wonder why.

You must choose to improve yourself. Don't let life control you; you have to control your life. Most people don't realize that they are simply living on autopilot and always wondering why things aren't going well. You must constantly be aware of your way of thinking. The next time another idea arises, pay attention to how you react to it and what your mind is telling you.

Read books, listen to audio programs, and read other positive and uplifting articles. Find ways to turn everything into a positive. Your mind must know what is right or wrong; it just depends on what you tell it. If you tell yourself something enough times, your brain will start to believe it. Then all you have to do is tell yourself better stories, and you'll be happier, more positive, and able to deal with any issues that may arise.

Your success is in your hands

Growth in life is what you define it to be. For your part, you could decide how to achieve financial freedom or a flexible work arrangement. Some people want to travel the world, while others just want to do what they are passionate about. Growth is not necessarily just wealth or recognition; it can also be personal fulfillment.

If you had to plan your perfect day, what would it look like? Would you sit on a bench and enjoy the sun, meet your favorite celebrity, or maybe see tons of progress in your life?

Why you want to learn how to succeed in life is up to you. Your parents, mentors, teachers, and friends may have their own definition of growth. But their definitions are not for you. Whatever makes you feel fulfilled and happy is what you should focus on when mastering the art of growth. Most people worry about how to be successful because we all want to feel important.

The search for a higher purpose makes you fight for survival and growth.

Although you may not feel like you have influenced others as much as you wanted, your life can still influence people in ways you couldn't imagine.

A growth goal helps you live a more purposeful life by pushing you to work a little harder, pursue growth, and succeed.

CONCLUSION

Remember, young entrepreneurs, doctors, counselors, and good citizens, these five steps are just the beginning of your journey toward personal growth. By establishing your growth, exploring careers, networking, being confident, and staying active, you are setting yourself up for a bright and successful future. Embrace each step, take action, and believe in yourself, for the possibilities are endless. Your path to greatness starts now!

www.ingramcontent.com/pod-product-compliance
Lightning Source LLC
Chambersburg PA
CBHW071027080526
44587CB00015B/2532